From Saturn to Glasgow
50 favourite poems by Edwin Morgan

ALSO BY EDWIN MORGAN FROM CARCANET

A Book of Lives
A.D. – a trilogy of plays on the life of Jesus
Cathures
Collected Poems
New Selected Poems
Virtual and other Realities

Translations
Beowulf
Collected Translations
Gilgamesh
Jean Racine, *Phaedra*
Edmond Rostand, *Cyrano de Bergerac*

ALSO BY EDWIN MORGAN FROM MARISCAT
Tales from Baron Munchausen
Hold Hands among the Atoms
Attila Jószef, *Sixty Poems*

From Saturn to Glasgow
50 favourite poems by Edwin Morgan

edited by Robyn Marsack & Hamish Whyte

CARCANET

SCOTTISH POETRY LIBRARY

By leaves we live

This selection first published in Great Britain in 2008 by the
Scottish Poetry Library
5 Crichton's Close
Edinburgh EH8 8DT
www.spl.org.uk

in association with
Carcanet Press Ltd
4th Floor, Alliance House
Cross Street
Manchester M2 7AQ
www.carcanet.co.uk

A CIP catalogue record for this book
is available from the British Library

ISBN 978 1 85754 983 6

The publishers acknowledge subsidy from the Scottish Arts Council and the
Aye Write Bank of Scotland Book Festival towards the publication of this volume.

Designed by Barrie Tullett, Lincoln
Text matter typeset in Kingfisher and Bliss
Printed and bound in England by SRP Ltd, Exeter

INTRODUCTION

If you asked fifty people to choose their favourite Edwin Morgan poems, you'd likely get fifty different answers. It would seem that picking fifty favourites is quite easy if you only ask fifty people. We asked many more than that, with nominations being open to *Herald* readers in particular, through the publicity in the paper and on its website, and on the Scottish Poetry Library's website and in libraries too — with the result that the book could have been twice the size ... but there were three or four poems that kept recurring: 'One Cigarette', for example ('It's so Audrey Hepburn — I love it!'), 'Strawberries' and 'Trio', which show Morgan as a great love poet, whether in the personal encounter or in celebration of the human capacity to love, epitomized for eternity in the trio walking up Buchanan Street. It was perhaps no accident that two laureates — Liz Lochhead and Andrew Motion — chose 'The First Men on Mercury' for its inventiveness and brio but also its serious messages about communication, translation and even colonisation. All the poems here were chosen as favourites, although some were nominated without reasons being given.

To our knowledge, this is the first time a collection of poems has been picked as a city-wide read, and who better to 'push out the boat' than Edwin Morgan, Glasgow's first poet laureate and then Scotland's, a poet of infinite variety, held in great affection by his native city and by writers and readers throughout Scotland. Glasgow's Aye Write annual book festival will be distributing 15,000 copies of this book free across the city, and we are thrilled to think of Morgan's poems dropping into the hands of those who already know and love them and of those who will encounter his work for the first time.

When we asked Edwin Morgan himself what he thought of the idea, he said, 'Daft!' — and then changed his mind — 'But good!' (with that characteristic twinkle in his eye). The selection offers many of the poems he would have expected to find in it, but also some unexpected entries such as 'Sunday in East Mars' and 'Boethius'. Asked to pick his own favourite, he eventually settled for 'Cinquevalli', but another day might have brought another answer: there's a Morgan poem for every mood and occasion.

This has sent us back to re-read Morgan's poems with renewed enthusiasm and delight, and with wonder at his seemingly endless inventiveness, the persistent curiosity and openness with which he views this world and imagined worlds, and his undimmed faith in the human. We're sure that whoever you are, you'll find at least one poem here that you'll want to carry with you for a long time to come.

Robyn Marsack & Hamish Whyte
St Andrew's Day 2007

LINKS/FURTHER READING
For more on Edwin Morgan, read:
About Edwin Morgan, eds Robert Crawford & Hamish Whyte (EUP, 1990)
Edwin Morgan, *Nothing Not Giving Messages*, ed. Hamish Whyte (Polygon, 1990)
or look at or contact:
www.EdwinMorgan.com (official website, run by Claudia Kraskiewicz)
www.lib.gla.ac.uk (Glasgow University Library, which holds the manuscripts of EM in the Special Collections Department – email: *special@lib.gla.ac.uk*)
www.mitchelllibrary.org (Mitchell Library, Glasgow, which holds the Edwin Morgan Collection in its Special Collections Department – includes manuscripts, books, photographs, ephemera and EM's library)
www.spl.org.uk (Scottish Poetry Library, Edinburgh — for everything on poetry – its Edwin Morgan Archive will open in 2009 — email: *inquiries@spl.org.uk*)
www.poetryarchive.org (recording of EM reading his poems)
www.ltscotland.org.uk (Learning and Teaching Scotland has an Edwin Morgan resource for schools)
www.carcanet.co.uk (Carcanet Press, Manchester, EM's main publisher)
hamish.whyte@btinternet.com (email address of EM's Scottish publisher, Mariscat Press, Edinburgh)
Other useful addresses:
www.ayewrite.com (Aye Write! is Glasgow's Book Festival, organized by Glasgow City Libraries)
www.stmungosmirrorball.co.uk (St Mungo's Mirrorball: Glasgow-based poetry network, organizing readings, events, etc.)
www.vitalsynz.co.uk (Vital Synz is a new poetry society in Glasgow and runs the Edwin Morgan International Poetry Competition)

AFTER A LECTURE

Last and most unexpected friend, do you know you overthrew me
In those first moments when you walked towards me in that lecture-
    room, not to undo me
But you did undo me, I was shaking, I felt that well-known spear go
    through me,
And when we talked my mind was racing like a computer to keep that
    contact sparking. What drew me
Was irreducible but recognisable – drythroat fragments, physical
    certainties, emanations and invasions so quick to imbue me
        And wound me with hope
        I swore I would cope
With whatever late late lifeline this man, whom I knew I loved, picked
    up and threw me.

Thank God we have Edwin Morgan to tell us how to live and keep on living. At 87 he   Kathleen Jamie
is still meeting the world with his daring, trickstery inventiveness. This poem is from
Love and a Life, written when he was 82, an energetic, uplifting series of 50 poems
about love. It's full of long lines and piled-up rhymes and energy. I'm half Edwin
Morgan's age. To have half his zest would be wonderful.

THE APPLE'S SONG

Tap me with your finger,
rub me with your sleeve,
hold me, sniff me, peel me
curling round and round
till I burst out white and cold
from my tight red coat
and tingle in your palm
as if I'd melt and breathe
a living pomander
waiting for the minute
of joy when you lift me
to your mouth and crush me
and in taste and fragrance
I race through your head
in my dizzy dissolve.

I sit in the bowl
in my cool corner
and watch you as you pass
smoothing your apron.
Are you thirsty yet?
My eyes are shining.

Hamish Whyte   The best comment on this sensuous ventriloquist turn is Edwin Morgan's own:
'Nothing is not giving messages.'

BOETHIUS

'Even the thrush, garrulous among the trees,
Caught and caged, and cosseted to please
A room of folk, regaled with frisky seeds,
Bells, mirrors, all the honey it needs,
Twinkling fingers, voices cooing it to sing,
If once through the windows the winds should bring
Shifting shadows of leaves, O how it rages,
It scatters the well-meant seeds, nothing assuages
Its longing for the wild woods and the sky,
Nothing can stop its cry,
And yet the kindly jailers wonder why.'

Silvas dulci voce susurrat. So wrote
Boethius, caged in Pavia,
how many years, in chains,
ex-senator, ex-orator, ex-everything,
dignities and dignity swiped off,
tears not wiped off,
groaning alone unheard
by Theodoric on his throne.
Grim in iron or gold or in iron and gold
Gothic kings will not be told
how to rule Rome. Romans
will not pack senates; Goths will.
Boethius, you stub your toe on iron.
You have stumbled into displeasure.
Fate must fulfil.
Take a cell, a shirt, a pen. Amen.

Not quite amen.
They gave him chains, they gave him pain.
But in candled darkness he wrote a book
to question fate, to challenge desolation.
Spiteless, Christless, working through
to a 'Yes' at last, in his late late Latin,
it gave a god a labyrinthine chance
to make a case for present suffering,
eternal sufferance. We look askance
at its title, *The Consolation of Philosophy*.

That was a bravado to pique Theodoric.
Theodoric the Great was out of patience.
Theodoric had not heard of judicial murder
but used it well, issued his order
for a little torture, then execution.
There is no such thing as philosophy.
There is no such thing as consolation.
Tyrants have lapis lazuli and porphyry.
Prisoners, the iron and gold of indignation.

Catherine Fowler   I like the cool elegance and restrained emotion of this poem. Morgan empathises with the mental anguish and complex emotions of Boethius, described in his *Consolations of Philosophy*, as he comes to terms with his unjust imprisonment and anticipated execution. I believe the poem has a message for our own society, where many people feel they are imprisoned either physically or metaphysically by circumstances beyond their control.

CANEDOLIA
AN OFF-CONCRETE SCOTCH FANTASIA

oa! hoy! awe! ba! mey!

who saw?
rhu saw rum. garve saw smoo. nigg saw tain. lairg saw lagg.
rigg saw eigg. largs saw haggs. tongue saw luss. mull saw yell.
stoer saw strone. drem saw muck. gask saw noss. unst saw cults.
echt saw banff. weem saw wick. trool saw twatt.

how far?
from largo to lunga from joppa to skibo from ratho to shona from
ulva to minto from tinto to tolsta from soutra to marsco from
braco to barra from alva to stobo from fogo to fada from gigha to
gogo from kelso to stroma from hirta to spango.

what is it like there?
och it's freuchie, it's faifley, it's wamphray, it's frandy, it's
sliddery.

what do you do?
we foindle and fungle, we bonkle and meigle and maxpoffle. we
scotstarvit, armit, wormit, and even whifflet. we play at crossstobs,
leuchars, gorbals, and finfan. we scavaig, and there's aye a bit of
tilquhilly. if it's wet, treshnish and mishnish.

what is the best of the country?
blinkbonny! airgold! thundergay!

and the worst?
scrishven, shiskine, scrabster, and snizort.

listen! what's that?
catacol and wauchope, never heed them.

tell us about last night
well, we had a wee ferintosh and we lay on the quiraing. it was
pure strontian!

but who was there?
petermoidart and craigenkenneth and cambusputtock and
ecclemuchty and corriehulish and balladolly and altnacanny and
clauchanvrechan and stronachlochan and auchenlachar and
tighnacrankie and tilliebruaich and killieharra and invervannach
and achnatudlem and machrishellach and inchtamurchan and
auchterfechan and kinlochculter and ardnawhallie and
invershuggle.

and what was the toast?
schiehallion! schiehallion! schiehallion!

CHRISTMAS EVE

Loneliness of city Christmas Eves –
with real stars up there – clear – and stars
on poles and wires across the street, and streaming
cars all dark with parcels, home
to families and the lighted window trees –

I sat down in the bus beside him – white jeans,
black jerkin, slumped with head nodding
in sleep, face hidden by long black hair, hands
tattooed on the four fingers ADEN 1967
and on the right hand five Christian crosses.
As the bus jerked, his hand fell on my knee,
stayed there, lay heavily and alive
with blue carvings from another world
and seemed to hold me like a claw,
unmoving. It moved. I rubbed my ear
to steal a glance at him, found him
stealing a glance at me. It was not
the jerking of the bus, it was a proposition.
He shook his hair back, and I saw his face
for the first time, unshaven, hardman, a warning
whether in Aden or Glasgow, but our eyes held
while that blue hand burned into my leg.
Half drunk, half sleeping – but half what, half what?
As his hand stirred again, my arm covered it
while the bus jolted round a corner.
'Don't ge' aff tae ah ge' aff.' – But the conductor
was watching, came up and shook him, looked at me.
My ticket was up, I had to leave him sprawled there
with that hand that now seemed so defenceless
lying on the seat I had left. Half down the stair
I looked back. The last thing I saw was Aden
and five blue crosses for five dead friends.

It was only fifteen minutes out of life
but I feel as if I was lifted by a whirlwind
and thrown down on some desert rocks to die
of dangers as always far worse lost than run.

Janice Galloway   *From Glasgow to Saturn* was the first book of poems by a living author I had ever
bought. I was eighteen and fresh out of school, desperate to get at the excitement of
the wider world, which meant, initially, Glasgow. 'Christmas Eve' has always stayed
with me, changed, turned itself around to show different facets. And the end, its idea
of 'dangers as always far worse lost than run' has haunted me since I read it, and helped
me want to face the darker side of things in my own life. And yes, I can recite it still.

CINQUEVALLI

Cinquevalli is falling, falling.
The shining trapeze kicks and flirts free,
solo performer at last.
The sawdust puffs up with a thump,
settles on a tangle of broken limbs.
St Petersburg screams and leans.
His pulse flickers with the gas-jets. He lives.

Cinquevalli has a therapy.
In his hospital bed, in his hospital chair
he holds a ball, lightly, lets it roll round his hand,
or grips it tight, gauging its weight and resistance,
begins to balance it, to feel its life attached to his
by will and knowledge, invisible strings
that only he can see. He throws it
from hand to hand, always different,
always the same, always
different, always the
same.
His muscles learn to think, his arms grow very strong.

Cinquevalli in sepia
looks at me from an old postcard: bundle of enigmas.
Half faun, half military man; almond eyes, curly hair,
conventional moustache; tights, and a tunic loaded
with embroideries, tassels, chains, fringes; hand on hip
with a large signet-ring winking at the camera
but a bull neck and shoulders and a cannon-ball
at his elbow as he stands by the posing pedestal;
half reluctant, half truculent,
half handsome, half absurd,
but let me see you forget him: not to be done.

Cinquevalli is a juggler.
In a thousand theatres, in every continent,
he is the best, the greatest. After eight years perfecting
he can balance one billiard ball on another billiard ball
on top of a cue on top of a third billiard ball
in a wine-glass held in his mouth. To those
who say the balls are waxed, or flattened,
he patiently explains the trick will only work
because the spheres are absolutely true.
There is no deception in him. He is true.

Cinquevalli is juggling with a bowler,
a walking-stick, a cigar, and a coin.
Who foresees? How to please.
The last time round, the bowler
flies to his head, the stick sticks in his hand,
the cigar jumps into his mouth, the coin
lands on his foot – ah, but
is kicked into his eye
and held there as the miraculous monocle
without which the portrait would be incomplete.

Cinquevalli is practising.
He sits in his dressing-room talking to some friends,
at the same time writing a letter with one hand
and with the other juggling four balls.
His friends think of demons, but
'You could all do this,' he says,
sealing the letter with a billiard ball.

Cinquevalli is on the high wire in Odessa.
The roof cracks, he is falling, falling
into the audience, a woman breaks his fall,
he cracks her like a flea, but lives.

Cinquevalli broods in his armchair in Brixton Road.
He reads in the paper about the shells whining
at Passchendaele, imagines the mud and the dead.
He goes to the window and wonders through that dark evening
what is happening in Poland where he was born.
His neighbours call him a German spy.
'Kestner, Paul Kestner, that's his name!'
'Keep Kestner out of the British music-hall!'
He frowns; it is cold; his fingers seem stiff and old.

Cinquevalli tosses up a plate of soup
and twirls it on his forefinger; not a drop spills.
He laughs, and well may he laugh
who can do that. The astonished table
breathe again, laugh too, think the world
a spinning thing that spills, for a moment, no drop.

Cinquevalli's coffin sways through Brixton
only a few months before the Armistice.
Like some trick they cannot get off the ground
it seems to burden the shuffling bearers, all their arms
cross-juggle that displaced person, that man
of balance, of strength, of delights and marvels,
in his unsteady box at last into the earth.

Twenty years ago I did a tour of Ireland with Eddie. He changed his set most nights   Andrew Greig
but read this every night – it clearly meant a lot to him, and for me became a deep
expression of aspects of himself, his inner life. I can still hear his voice, those quick
peppery rhythms, his delight.

THE COALS

Before my mother's hysterectomy
she cried, and told me she must never bring
coals in from the cellar outside the house,
someone must do it for her. The thing itself
I knew was nothing, it was the thought
of that dependence. Her tears shocked me
like a blow. As once she had been taught,
I was taught self-reliance, discipline,
which is both good and bad. You get things done,
you feel you keep the waste and darkness back
by acts and acts and acts and acts and acts,
bridling if someone tells you this is vain,
learning at last in pain. Hardest of all
is to forgive yourself for things undone,
guilt that can poison life – away with it,
you say, and it is loath to go away.
I learned both love and joy in a hard school
and treasure them like the fierce salvage of
some wreck that has been built to look like stone
and stand, though it did not, a thousand years.

Diana Hendry   It's for the middle lines that I treasure this poem, because it brought both the recognition and comfort that I wasn't alone in attempting to 'keep the waste and darkness back'. I like the tender portrait of the poet's mother and the way the poem opens out to include the reader. And who but Morgan would dare to begin a poem with the blunt fact of a hysterectomy?

THE COIN

We brushed the dirt off, held it to the light.
The obverse showed us *Scotland*, and the head
of a red deer; the antler-glint had fled
but the fine cut could still be felt. All right:
we turned it over, read easily *One Pound*,
but then the shock of Latin, like a gloss,
Respublica Scotorum, sent across
such ages as we guessed but never found
at the worn edge where once the date had been
and where as many fingers had gripped hard
as hopes their silent race had lost or gained.
The marshy scurf crept up to our machine,
sucked at our boots. Yet nothing seemed ill-starred.
And least of all the realm the coin contained.

Sonnets from Scotland (1984) was a hugely uplifting read during a politically   James Robertson
frustrating time. Morgan seemed to reinvent Scotland's past, present and future.
In 'The Coin' space travellers find a coin, a relic from a country that once existed
– Scotland, but not a Scotland that has ever yet been. The poem asks if this is a
Scotland that *we* can attain? How long will it last? But there is a great optimism in
the last lines which still fill me with hope and pleasure whenever I read them.

COLUMBA'S SONG

Where's Brude? Where's Brude?
So many souls to be saved!
The bracken is thick, the wildcat is quick,
the foxes dance in the moonlight,
the salmon dance in the waters,
the adders dance in the thick brown bracken.
Where's Brude? Where's man?
There's too much nature here,
eagles and deer,
but where's the mind and where's the soul?
Show me your kings, your women, the man of the plough.
And cry me to your cradles.
It wasn't for a fox or an eagle I set sail!

Michael Schmidt   I loved 'Columba's Song' when I saw it in the manuscript of *From Glasgow to Saturn*, the first book Edwin submitted to Carcanet, published two-thirds of my life ago. It stuck in my memory, the bold faux-Romantic opening, and then the phrase, 'there's too much nature here', one of the flares this great explorer sent up to illuminate his vast peopled cityscapes, and one of the stars he shot up to enrich the galaxy.

THE COMPUTER'S FIRST CHRISTMAS CARD

```
j o l l y m e r r y
h o l l y b e r r y
j o l l y b e r r y
m e r r y h o l l y
h a p p y j o l l y
j o l l y j e l l y
j e l l y b e l l y
b e l l y m e r r y
h o l l y h e p p y
j o l l y M o l l y
m a r r y J e r r y
m e r r y H a r r y
h o p p y B a r r y
h e p p y J a r r y
b o p p y h e p p y
b e r r y j o r r y
j o r r y j o l l y
m o p p y j e l l y
M o l l y m e r r y
J e r r y j o l l y
b e l l y b o p p y
j o r r y h o p p y
h o l l y m o p p y
B a r r y m e r r y
J a r r y h a p p y
h a p p y b o p p y
b o p p y j o l l y
j o l l y m e r r y
m e r r y m e r r y
m e r r y m e r r y
m e r r y C h r i s
a m m e r r y a s a
C h r i s m e r r y
a s M E R R Y C H R
Y S A N T H E M U M
```

The first Morgan poem I ever encountered. I was probably 13 or 14. It was my first taste of concrete poetry. It was also very funny with an excellent punchline, and it looked to technology and the future (not at that time, as far as I was aware, concerns of poets). Even today, it puts a smile on my face.

Ian Rankin

DEATH IN DUKE STREET

A huddle on the greasy street –
cars stop, nose past, withdraw –
dull glint on soles of tackety boots,
frayed rough blue trousers, nondescript coat
stretching back, head supported
in strangers' arms, a crowd collecting –
'Whit's wrang?' 'Can ye see'm?'
'An auld fella, he's had it.'
On one side, a young mother in a headscarf
is kneeling to comfort him, her three-year-old son
stands puzzled, touching her coat, her shopping-bag
spills its packages that people look at
as they look at everything. On the other side
a youth, nervous, awkwardly now
at the centre of attention as he shifts his arm
on the old man's shoulders, wondering
what to say to him, glancing up at the crowd.
These were next to him when he fell,
and must support him into death.
He seems not to be in pain,
he is speaking slowly and quietly
but he does not look at any of them,
his eyes are fixed on the sky,
already he is moving out
beyond everything belonging.
As if he still belonged
they hold him very tight.

Only the hungry ambulance
howls for him through the staring squares.

Louise Welsh   I walk along Duke Street often and can see this scene plainly in my head. This is not
the way any of us would like to go, collapsing on the pavement among the shoppers.
But the bystanders' compassion and tenderness, their acceptance that they must
usher the old stranger into death is beautiful. There is something biblical about the
image. Stanley Spencer could have done a wonderful painting of it.

THE DEATH OF MARILYN MONROE

25

What innocence? Whose guilt? What eyes? Whose breast?
Crumpled orphan, nembutal bed,
white hearse, Los Angeles,
DiMaggio! Los Angeles! Miller! Los Angeles! America!
That Death should seem the only protector –
That all arms should have faded, and the great cameras and lights
    become an inquisition and a torment –
That the many acquaintances, the autograph-hunters, the
    inflexible directors, the drive-in admirers should become
    a blur of incomprehension and pain –
That lonely Uncertainty should limp up, grinning, with
    bewildering barbiturates, and watch her undress and lie
    down and in her anguish
call for him! call for him to strengthen her with what could
    only dissolve her! A method
of dying, we are shaken, we see it. Strasberg!
Los Angeles! Olivier! Los Angeles! Others die
and yet by this death we are a little shaken, we feel it,
America.
Let no one say communication is a cantword.
They had to lift her hand from the bedside telephone.
But what she had not been able to say
perhaps she had said. 'All I had was my life.
I have no regrets, because if I made
any mistakes, I was responsible.
There is now – and there is the future.
What has happened is behind. So
it follows you around? So what?' – This
to a friend, ten days before.
And so she was responsible.
And if she was not responsible, not wholly responsible, Los Angeles?
    Los Angeles? Will it follow you around? Will the slow
    white hearse of the child of America follow you around?

This fairly thrums with painful feelings in its portrayal of the unhappy star's   Liz Young
victimisation by Hollywood. The poem's soaring protest at her tragic end always
leaves me stunned.

A DEMON

My job is to rattle the bars. It's a battle.
The gates are high, large, long, hard, black.
Whatever the metal is, it is asking to be struck.
There are guards of course, but I am very fast
And within limits I can change my shape.
The dog watches me, but I am not trying
To get out; nor am I trying to get in.
He growls if I lift my iron shaft.
I smile at that, and with a sudden whack
I drag it lingeringly and resoundingly
Along the gate; then he's berserk: fine!

The peeling miasma of the underworld
Is perfectly visible through the palings,
Grey, cold, dank, with what might be willows,
What might be villas, open caves, wildfire,
Thrones, amphitheatres, shades walking,
Shades gathering, and yes, there he is, the Orph,
The orphan, Orpheus, picking at his harp
On Pluto's glimmery piazza, the voice,
The tenderer of hope, the high-note
Shiverer of goblets, the spellbinder,
The author of what might be, surely not,
A shining wetness at the corner of Pluto's eye.
My time has come! I scramble like a monkey
From stake to stake and spar to spar and rattle
My rod, a ratchet for the rungs, a grating
Of something from gratings that has nutmegged,
Pungenced, punched, punctuated the singing
And made the singer devilish angry,
Devilish fearful, and at last devilish strong.
The vizors are after me. Too late, grey ones!
I've done my bit. Orpheus is learning along.

Willie Hershaw   The title poem of the *Demon* sequence, where the demon visits the Underworld and deliberately creates mayhem, including interrupting the harping of Orpheus with his racket (great line: 'my job is to rattle the bars'), says a lot about Morgan's own attitude to poetry/art – challenging, a sense of devilment, erudite, always unexpected, out to cowp the Establishment.

THE FIRST MEN ON MERCURY

–We come in peace from the third planet.
 Would you take us to your leader?

–Bawr stretter! Bawr. Bawr. Stretterhawl?

–This is a little plastic model
 of the solar system, with working parts.
 You are here and we are there and we
 are now here with you, is this clear?

–Gawl horrop. Bawr Abawrhannahanna!

–Where we come from is blue and white
 with brown, you see we call the brown
 here 'land', the blue is 'sea', and the white
 is 'clouds' over land and sea, we live
 on the surface of the brown land,
 all round is sea and clouds. We are 'men'.
 Men come –

–Glawp men! Gawrbenner menko. Menhawl?

–Men come in peace from the third planet
 which we call 'earth'. We are earthmen.
 Take us earthmen to your leader.

–Thmen? Thmen? Bawr. Bawrhossop.
 Yuleeda tan hanna. Harrabost yuleeda.

–I am the yuleeda. You see my hands,
 we carry no benner, we come in peace.
 The spaceways are all stretterhawn.

–Glawn peacemen all horrabhanna tantko!
 Tan come at'mstrossop. Glawp yuleeda!

–Atoms are peacegawl in our harraban.
Menbat worrabost from tan hannahanna.

–You men we know bawrhossoptant. Bawr.
We know yuleeda. Go strawg backspetter quick.

–We cantantabawr, tantingko backspetter now!

–Banghapper now! Yes, third planet back.
Yuleeda will go back blue, white, brown
nowhanna! There is no more talk.

–Gawl han fasthapper?

–No. You must go back to your planet.
Go back in peace, take what you have gained
but quickly.

–Stretterworra gawl, gawl...

–Of course, but nothing is ever the same,
now is it? You'll remember Mercury.

Andrew Motion   It's hard to choose a single poem to celebrate Edwin's poetry, since its power
depends in important ways on its abundance. Eventually I've plumped for 'The
First Men on Mercury', which is itself a kind of poetic cornucopia – adventurous,
transgressive, fun (but serious too), and stamped with a mark of imaginative
boldness which is vintage Morgan.

THE FLOWERS OF SCOTLAND

Yes, it is too cold in Scotland for flower people; in any case who would
    be handed a thistle?
What are our flowers? Locked swings and private rivers –
and the island of Staffa for sale in the open market, which no one
    questions or thinks strange –
and lads o' pairts that run to London and Buffalo without a backward
    look while their elders say Who'd blame them –
and bonny fechters kneedeep in dead ducks with all the thrawn
    intentness of the incorrigible professional Scot –
and a Kirk Assembly that excels itself in the bad old rhetoric and tries
    to stamp out every glow of charity and change, most wrong
    when it thinks most loudly it is most right –
and a Scottish National Party that refuses to discuss Vietnam and is
    even applauded for doing so, do they think no lesson is to be
    learned from what is going on there? –
and the unholy power of Grouse-moor and Broad-acres to prevent
    the smoke of useful industry from sullying Invergordon or
    setting up linear cities among the whaups –
and the banning of Beardsley and Joyce but not of course of 'Monster
    on the Campus' or 'Curse of the Undead' – those who think the
    former are the more degrading, what are their values?
and the steady creep of the preservationist societies, wearing their pens
    out for slums with good leaded lights – if they could buy all the
    amber in the Baltic and melt it over Edinburgh would they be
    happy then? – the skeleton is well-proportioned –
and by contrast the massive indifference to the slow death of the Clyde
    estuary, decline of resorts, loss of steamers, anaemia of yachting,
    cancer of monstrous installations of a foreign power and an
    acquiescent government – what is the smell of death on a child's
    spade, any more than rats to leaded lights? –
and dissidence crying in the wilderness to a moor of boulders and
    two ospreys –
these are the flowers of Scotland.

Unlike a lot of Edwin Morgan's work, this poem is not high on subtlety. It initially   Peter McNally
seems quite dated but on re-reading it is hugely contemporary. There are a lot
of elements specific to Scotland but the ideas transcend nation and highlight
dishonourable leadership and a whole lot more.

THE FRESHET

Will you not brush me again, rhododendron?
You were blowsy with rainwater when you drenched my cheek,
I might have been weeping, but was only passing, too
quickly! You were so heavy and wet and fresh
I thought your purple must run, make me a Pict.
You made yourself a sponge for me, I got
a shower, a shot, a spray, a freshet, a headstart
and then I was away from you. I can't go back.
I can't go back, you know, retrace my steps,
tilt my other cheek out like an idiot,
stumble purposefully against the blooms
for another heady shiver. I want it though!

One day when I am not thinking, walking
steadily past house and garden, measuring
the traffic lights, you will reach out, won't you,
at a corner, toppling over railings
just to see me, crowd of mauve raindrops
shaking and bursting, mauling me gently
with your petal paws, shock of the petal,
shock of the water, I am waiting for that,
out of I don't care how many pavements,
black railings, and the darkly breathing green.

FROM A CITY BALCONY

How often when I think of you the day grows bright!
Our silent love
wanders in Glen Fruin with butterflies and cuckoos –
bring me the drowsy country thing! Let it drift above the traffic
by the open window with a cloud of witnesses –
a sparkling burn, white lambs, the blaze of gorse,
the cuckoos calling madly, the real white clouds over us,
white butterflies about your hand in the short hot grass,
and then the witness was my hand closing on yours,
my mouth brushing your eyelids and your lips
again and again till you sighed and turned for love.
Your breast and thighs were blazing like the gorse.
I covered your great fire in silence there.
We let the day grow old along the grass.
It was in the silence the love was.

Footsteps and witnesses! In this Glasgow balcony who pours
such joy like mountain water? It brims, it spills over and over
down to the parched earth and the relentless wheels.
How often will I think of you, until
our dying steps forget this light, forget
that we ever knew the happy glen,
or that I ever said, We must jump into the sun,
and we jumped into the sun.

I love how this poem gives the reader everything: the city, the country, the past, the present. Euphoria, sadness, men and butterflies! It makes me think of the young Morgan in love and the old one simultaneously – a Morgan poem can easily span time. A few jumps into the sun. It is all about the way memory works – as if at the exact moment love was blazing in the gorse, it was already becoming a memory.

Jackie Kay

GLASGOW 5 MARCH 1971

With a ragged diamond
of shattered plate-glass
a young man and his girl
are falling backwards into a shop-window.
The young man's face
is bristling with fragments of glass
and the girl's leg has caught
on the broken window
and spurts arterial blood
over her wet-look white coat.
Their arms are starfished out
braced for impact,
their faces show surprise, shock,
and the beginning of pain.
The two youths who have pushed them
are about to complete the operation
reaching into the window
to loot what they can smartly.
Their faces show no expression.
It is a sharp clear night
in Sauchiehall Street.
In the background two drivers
keep their eyes on the road.

G.M. HOPKINS IN GLASGOW
FOR J.A.M.R.

33

Earnestly nervous yet forthright, melted
by bulk and warmth and unimposed rough grace,
he lit a ready fuse from face to face
of Irish Glasgow. Dark tough tight-belted
drunken Fenian poor ex-Ulstermen
crouched round a brazier like a burning bush
and lurched into his soul with such a push
that British angels blanched in mid-amen
to see their soldier stumble like a Red.
Industry's pauperism singed his creed.
He blessed them, frowned, beat on his hands. The load
of coal-black darkness clattering on his head
half-crushed, half-fed the bluely burning need
that trudged him back along North Woodside Road.

This renders in fierce imagery the impact the harsh life of Irish immigrants had on the poet Gerard Manley Hopkins, who came to Glasgow in 1871. The dark is there – but so is the spark and the lyrical power that comes from tuning in to the pain of the dispossessed. The poem has a personal resonance, as my Irish grandfather, born 1871, came to the city as a young man and slept in doorways till he could get digs.

Willie Maley

HYENA

I am waiting for you.
I have been travelling all morning through the bush
and not eaten.
I am lying at the edge of the bush
on a dusty path that leads from the burnt-out kraal.
I am panting, it is midday, I found no water-hole.
I am very fierce without food and although my eyes
are screwed to slits against the sun
you must believe I am prepared to spring.

What do you think of me?
I have a rough coat like Africa.
I am crafty with dark spots
like the bush-tufted plains of Africa.
I sprawl as a shaggy bundle of gathered energy
like Africa sprawling in its waters.
I trot, I lope, I slaver, I am a ranger.
I hunch my shoulders. I eat the dead.

Do you like my song?
When the moon pours hard and cold on the veldt
I sing, and I am the slave of darkness.
Over the stone walls and the mud walls and the ruined places
and the owls, the moonlight falls.
I sniff a broken drum. I bristle. My pelt is silver.
I howl my song to the moon – up it goes.
Would you meet me there in the waste places?

It is said I am a good match
for a dead lion. I put my muzzle
at his golden flanks, and tear. He
is my golden supper, but my tastes are easy.
I have a crowd of fangs, and I use them.
Oh and my tongue – do you like me
when it comes lolling out over my jaw
very long, and I am laughing?
I am not laughing.
But I am not snarling either, only
panting in the sun, showing you
what I grip
carrion with.

I am waiting
for the foot to slide,
for the heart to seize,
for the leaping sinews to go slack,
for the fight to the death to be fought to the death,
for a glazing eye and the rumour of blood.
I am crouching in my dry shadows
till you are ready for me.
My place is to pick you clean
and leave your bones to the wind.

I love his animal poems and I love the way in this poem he inhabits so effortlessly the creature itself, his uneasy questioning of the reader or potential victim coupled with the unsettling powerful 'I' voice – 'I hunch the shoulders, I eat the dead' – and finally, 'My place is to pick you clean and leave your bones to the wind'. Scary stuff!

Jim Carruth

IN THE SNACK-BAR

A cup capsizes along the formica,
slithering with a dull clatter.
A few heads turn in the crowded evening snack-bar.
An old man is trying to get to his feet
from the low round stool fixed to the floor.
Slowly he levers himself up, his hands have no power.
He is up as far as he can get. The dismal hump
looming over him forces his head down.
He stands in his stained beltless gaberdine
like a monstrous animal caught in a tent
in some story. He sways slightly,
the face not seen, bent down
in shadow under his cap.
Even on his feet he is staring at the floor
or would be, if he could see.
I notice now his stick, once painted white
but scuffed and muddy, hanging from his right arm.
Long blind, hunchback born, half paralysed
he stands
fumbling with the stick
and speaks:
'I want – to go to the – toilet.'

It is down two flights of stairs, but we go.
I take his arm. 'Give me – your arm – it's better,' he says.
Inch by inch we drift towards the stairs.
A few yards of floor are like a landscape
to be negotiated, in the slow setting out
time has almost stopped. I concentrate
my life to his: crunch of spilt sugar,
slidy puddle from the night's umbrellas,
table edges, people's feet,
hiss of the coffee-machine, voices and laughter,
smell of a cigar, hamburgers, wet coats steaming,
and the slow dangerous inches to the stairs.

I put his right hand on the rail
and take his stick. He clings to me. The stick
is in his left hand, probing the treads.
I guide his arm and tell him the steps.
And slowly we go down. And slowly we go down.
White tiles and mirrors at last. He shambles
uncouth into the clinical gleam.
I set him in position, stand behind him
and wait with his stick.
His brooding reflection darkens the mirror
but the trickle of his water is thin and slow,
an old man's apology for living.
Painful ages to close his trousers and coat –
I do up the last buttons for him.
He asks doubtfully, 'Can I – wash my hands?'
I fill the basin, clasp his soft fingers round the soap.
He washes, feebly, patiently. There is no towel.
I press the pedal of the drier, draw his hands
gently into the roar of the hot air.
But he cannot rub them together,
drags out a handkerchief to finish.
He is glad to leave the contraption, and face the stairs.
He climbs, and steadily enough.
He climbs, we climb. He climbs
with many pauses but with that one
persisting patience of the undefeated
which is the nature of man when all is said.
And slowly we go up. And slowly we go up.
The faltering, unfaltering steps
take him at last to the door
across that endless, yet not endless waste of floor.
I watch him helped on a bus. It shudders off in the rain.
The conductor bends to hear where he wants to go.

Wherever he could go it would be dark
and yet he must trust men.
Without embarrassment or shame
he must announce his most pitiful needs
in a public place. No one sees his face.
Does he know how frightening he is in his strangeness
under his mountainous coat, his hands like wet leaves
stuck to the half-white stick?
His life depends on many who would evade him.
But he cannot reckon up the chances,
having one thing to do,
to haul his blind hump through these rains of August.
Dear Christ, to be born for this!

Stuart Murdoch   The main reason this is my favourite is that 'we got it in school'. At the time I thought that this was the grimmest of set texts, but phrases stayed with me, and when I read it now I must admit that it makes tears well, half from the humanity, half that recognises the God-given skill of the poet.

INSTRUCTIONS TO AN ACTOR

Now, boy, remember this is the great scene.
You'll stand on a pedestal behind a curtain,
the curtain will be drawn, and then you don't move
for eighty lines; don't move, don't speak, don't breathe.
I'll stun them all out there, I'll scare them,
make them weep, but it depends on you.
I warn you eighty lines is a long time,
but you don't breathe, you're dead,
you're a dead queen, a statue,
you're dead as stone, new-carved,
new-painted and the paint not dry
– we'll get some red to keep your lip shining –
and you're a mature woman, you've got dignity,
some beauty still in middle age, and
you're kind and true, but you're dead,
your husband thinks you're dead,
the audience thinks you're dead,
and you don't breathe, boy, I say
you don't even blink for eighty lines,
if you blink you're out!
Fix your eye on something and keep watching it.
Practise when you get home. It can be done.
And you move at last – music's the cue.
When you hear a mysterious solemn jangle
of instruments, make yourself ready.
Five lines more, you can lift a hand.
It may tingle a bit, but lift it –
slow, slow –
O this is where I hit them
right between the eyes, I've got them now –
I'm making the dead walk –
you move a foot, slow, steady, down,
you guard your balance in case you're stiff,
you move, you step down, down from the pedestal,
control your skirt with one hand, the other hand

you now hold out –
O this will melt their hearts if nothing does –
to your husband who wronged you long ago
and hesitates in amazement
to believe you are alive.
Finally he embraces you, and there's nothing
I can give you to say, boy,
but you must show that you have forgiven him.
Forgiveness, that's the thing. It's like a second life.
I know you can do it. – Right then, shall we try?

Ali Smith   This single poem gets, via the heart of all theatre, to the heart of the communal in all
the arts, and to the heart of form, the heart of voice and of silence and to the heart
of a kind of life that will never actually stop. That's what Morgan does, he gets to the
heart of the heart, selflessly, wide-openly, with the joyous shock of energy that's the
core heartbeat of life-form and art-form.

JOHN TENNANT

Tennant's Stalk - that's my monument.
Talk of the town, top of the walk, tells them to stop,
Any that trudge by that well-named Sight Hill.
It tapers elegant to its hourly bloom,
Thick smoke, acrid, highest anywhere,
Four hundred and thirty blessed feet
Above my empire, my chemical, empire,
My blessed St Rollox, biggest anywhere,
My eighty acres of evenhandedly
Distributing industry and desolation!.
Chief of all chimneys, carry your noxiousness
Into the clouds and away from my employees,
Settling if it must where I cannot see it!
I am in business for the uses of the world,
Bleaching powder, soap, sulphuric acid,
A thousand casks a week from my cooperage.
I'm standing here in the midst of furnaces .
Which I understand and command - oh yes,
If there is anything new or strange in chemistry
It will not be the case that I have not heard of it.

Boasting, in my Glasgow way? Well, perhaps.
I am a chemist with passions. I am a character,
They say. Take my wife. I don't mean take my wife,
But just consider. We are not married
Except by good old Scottish cohabitation.
She is a total non-person to my family.
My brother, well we don't get on, that's that.
My sister-in-law, put bluntly, is a bitch.
My dear Rosina was a factory girl,
She may be beautiful, she may be bright -
She *is* beautiful, she *is* bright -
But a lassie from St Rollox, that's not on.
Well well, I've put their gas in a peep,
That claque or clat of bitches who can't stand

Class mix - my grand house in West George Street
Has, or should I say boasts, a fine brass plate
For MR & MRS JOHN TENNANT. And that's us.

How can a rebel be a capitalist?
What's the problem? I have a yacht - of *course*! -
And some have tried to poach my butler - fat chance -
But who was it marched through Glasgow in '32
To see the great Reform Bill safely through?
Who was it planted a doctor in the works
To give free treatment to all? Who ran
A factory school for workers' weans? Who
Cranked up mechanics' institutes? Who stayed
In the centre of Glasgow when the nabobs and nobs
Hustled out to suburban palazzos?
I'm bluff and gruff and tough enough,
If a foreman is a pain in the arse
I tell him he's a pain in the arse.
My eyebrows are bushy, and if my finger is in my fob
You had better watch out if you are skiving your job.
But, or rather BUT,
If ever you are down on your luck
You can come to me, you can run
With a secret misery, I can cut
Corners for you, nothing is shut
That John Tennant cannot get unstuck.

I come back to my Stalk, my obelisk, my watchtower,
My beautiful slender avant-garde polluter.
What poet would sing those acres of grey ash,
That ghastly guff of hydrogen sulphide?
Who cares? I'm happy to stand in for Homer.
His gods would have cackled with joy
To see my new-born boy
Poking manfully towards their heavenly rookery.

I marked the occasion - oh, did I not!
I gathered a posse of friends to hansel the Stalk.
Ladies and gents, I said, you're going to the top!
Such cries of horror, it was like a play.
I relished the moment, lifted a hand
For the clamour to subside. Just a joke, folks.
I don't need steeplejacks. It's *inside* you're going.
The bricks are the best money can buy,
They are new, they are brilliant, not a smitch of soot.
Please admire them as you rise past them.

Climb? Not a step. You will mount like magic
By a system of hissing steam-powered pulleys -
O James blessed Watt, late of this parish! -
Emerge at the viewing platform, safe as houses,
And sweep your eyes around like modern gods.
What's that sir? Insurance? Christ man
This is Glasgow. You are pioneers. Get in.
There's a woman in the Stalk before you.
Yes ma'am? Skirts? That's taken care of.
No one will look up your furbelows.
The ladies will sit in a basket, like balloonists.
The gents will be in buckets, like Brahmins.

Well, up they went into the half dark,
Clutching their ropes, listening to the pulley,
Silenced by the mystery.
The summit was all light and air and chatter.
The smoky city was shunting fiercely below
But the height, the horizon, the haze was their hope
As they looked at, looked for, Scotland.
The firth, the masts and sails, the Arran hills,
The river winding south through glasshouses,
Eastward a faint glint of spires - Edinburgh?
We don't want Edinburgh! Find Ben Lomond!

They found it, and they found much else
As they leaned on my parapet, not paradise
But a throb of the great paradox,
Useful filth, mitigated pain,
Crops of brick and iron, with or without rain.

KING BILLY

Grey over Riddrie the clouds piled up,
dragged their rain through the cemetery trees.
The gates shone cold. Wind rose
flaring the hissing leaves, the branches
swung, heavy, across the lamps.
Gravestones huddled in drizzling shadow,
flickering streetlight scanned the requiescats,
a name and an urn, a date, a dove
picked out, lost, half-regained.
What is this dripping wreath, blown from its grave
red, white, blue, and gold
'To Our Leader of Thirty Years Ago' –

Bareheaded, in dark suits, with flutes
and drums, they brought him here, in procession
seriously, King Billy of Brigton, dead,
from Bridgeton Cross: a memory of violence,
brooding days of empty bellies,
billiard smoke and a sour pint,
boots or fists, famous sherrickings,
the word, the scuffle, the flash, the shout,
bloody crumpling in the close,
bricks for papish windows, get
the Conks next time, the Conks ambush
the Billy Boys, the Billy Boys the Conks till
Sillitoe scuffs the razors down the stank –
No, but it isn't the violence they remember
but the legend of a violent man
born poor, gang-leader in the bad times
of idleness and boredom, lost in better days,
a bouncer in a betting club,
a quiet man at last, dying
alone in Bridgeton in a box bed.
So a thousand people stopped the traffic
for the hearse of a folk hero and the flutes

threw 'Onward Christian Soldiers' to the winds
from unironic lips, the mourners kept
in step, and there were some who wept.

Go from the grave. The shrill flutes
are silent, the march dispersed.
Deplore what is to be deplored,
and then find out the rest.

Andrew MacLean Apart from the genius of the poem – the historical detail is wonderful – the closing
lines for me sum up so many issues in life: 'Deplore what is to be deplored, / and then
find out the rest.' The poem rings true.

THE LOCH NESS MONSTER'S SONG

Sssnnnwhuffffll?
Hnwhuffl hhnnwfl hnfl hfl?
Gdroblboblhobngbl gbl gl g g g g glbgl.
Drublhaflablhaflubhafgabhaflhafl fl fl –
gm grawwwww grf grawf awfgm graw gm.
Hovoplodok-doplodovok-plovodokot-doplodokosh?
Splgraw fok fok splgrafhatchgabrlgabrl fok splfok!
Zgra kra gka fok!
Grof grawff gahf?
Gombl mbl bl –
blm plm,
blm plm,
blm plm,
blp.

My reasons for nominating this poem: Tom Malone
Bkshhhffllt remmimblsh mi mi mi mifll / Awfll da luvllll liki k k k ugh ndri fokof
Gll gll glluch Nssssssss n / Splshli di vllllg awv / Drm / Na / Drrrrrrch / ut
mmmmmmmmh!

LINES FOR WALLACE

Is it not better to forget?
It is better not to forget.
Betrayal never to be forgotten,
Vindictiveness never to be forgotten,
Triumphalism never to be forgotten.
Body parts displayed
At different points of the compass,
Between hanging and hacking
The worst, the disembowelling.
Blood raised in him, fervent,
Blood raced in him, fervent,
Blood razed in him, for ever
Fervent in its death.
For Burns was right to see
It was not only in the field
That Scots would follow this man
With blades and war-horns
Sharp and shrill
But with brains and books
Where the idea of liberty
Is impregnated and impregnates.
Oh that too is sharp and shrill
And some cannot stand it
And some would never allow it
And some would rather die
For the regulated music
Of Zamyatin's Polyhymnia
Where nothing can go wrong.
Cinema sophisticates
Fizzed with disgust at the crudities
Braveheart held out to them.
Over the cheeks of some
(Were they less sophisticated?)
A tear slipped unbidden.
Oh yes it did. I saw it.

The power of Wallace
Cuts through art
But art calls attention to it
Badly or well.
In your room, in the street
Even by god if it came to it,
On a battlefield,
Think about it,
Remember him.

I nominate the lines Morgan wrote for the 700th anniversary of the execution of Sir William Wallace. The spontaneous language forcibly reminds us both of the horrific event, and of how the story of Wallace has inspired generations of Scots fighting for liberty, whether on battlefields or in debating chambers.

David Brown

MAKING A POEM

Coming in with it
from frost and buses
gently burning
you must prepare it
with luck
to go critical.
Give the hook your scarf,
the chrome hook, maybe,
your green scarf. Say
Smoky Smoky
to the cat, set him
on his cushion, perhaps
a patch cushion
from old Perth.
Put the kettle on,
go to the window,
mist the glass
dreaming a minute lightly,
boys on the ice,
rows of orange lamps.
And go cut
white new bread.
Make tea like skaters' leaves.
You're never free.
It's blue dark night again.
Below the panes
in quietness.
Take a pencil
like the milkman's horse
round and round.
But you must agree
with it, and love it,
even when it grows
too fierce for favour.
It comes, and the cat shines.
And make the poem now.

MATT MCGINN

We cannot see it, it keeps changing so.
All round us, *in and out, above, below,*
at evening, phantom figures come and go,
silently, *just a magic shadow show.*
A hoarse voice singing *come love watch with me*
was all we heard on that fog-shrouded bank.
We thought we saw him, but if so, he sank
into the irrecoverable sea.
Dear merry man, what is your country now?
Does it keep changing? Will we ever see it?
A crane, a backcourt, an accordion?
Or sherbet dabs, henna, and jasmined brow?
The book is clasped, and time will never free it.
Mektub. The caravan winds jangling on.

Matt wrote the song 'Magic Shadow Show' for his brother, using lines from Adam McNaughtan
Fitzgerald's *Rubaiyat of Omar Khayyam* but his own early death gave it another
resonance. Edwin wove the lines of the song into his sonnet, examining similarities
between the Calton merryman and the Persian poet. The suggestion that Matt
might now be singing on 'another bank and shoal of time' gives way to the notion,
closer to Omar's philosophy, that the book is clasped and life's caravan goes on
without the dead singer.

MESSAGE CLEAR

```
             am              i
                                    if
         i am                  he
             he r        o
             h    ur   t
             the re          and
             he     re   and
             he re
         a              n   d
             the r              e
         i am    r                 ife
                     i n
                 s      ion and
         i                 d    i e
           am   e res   ect
           am   e res   ection
                          o         f
             the                 life
                          o         f
           m    e         n
                 sur e
             the              d    i e
         i        s
                 s    e t    and
         i am the  sur         d
           a   t   res    t
                          o         life
         i am  he r                 e
         i a           ct
         i     r   u     n
         i  m   e e      t
         i            t          i e
         i       s    t    and
         i am th         o    th
         i am    r           a
```

```
i am the  su      n
i am the  s     on
i am the  e   rect on      e if
i am    re        n    t
i am    s        a        fe
i am     s   e   n    t
i    he e             d
i    t e  s    t
i       re        a d
  a   th re        a d
  a      s    t on      e
  a   t  re        a d
  a   th r      on      e
i       resurrect
                  a      life
i am           i  n      life
i am    resurrection
i am the resurrection and
i am
i am the resurrection and the life
```

Morgan, as so often, plays a game with words yet meditates on a vast and serious theme. Beginning with 'am I / I am if', the form of the poem in its gaps and hesitations, its uncertainties and repetitive certainties, mimics the whole stuttering process of coming to the great recognition of the closing line: 'I am the resurrection and the life'. The message emerges, and it is clear.

Robyn Marsack

MIDGE

The evening is perfect, my sisters.
The loch lies silent, the air is still.
The sun's last rays linger over the water
and there is a faint smirr, almost a smudge
of summer rain. Sisters, I smell supper,
and what is more perfect than supper?
It is emerging from the wood,
in twos and threes, a dozen in all,
making such a chatter and a clatter
as it reaches the rocky shore,
admiring the arrangements of the light.
See the innocents, my sisters,
the clumsy ones, the laughing ones,
the rolled-up sleeves and the flapping shorts,
there is even a kilt (god of the midges,
you are good to us!) So gather your forces,
leave your tree-trunks, forsake the rushes,
fly up from the sour brown mosses
to the sweet flesh of face and forearm.
Think of your eggs. What does the egg need?
Blood, and blood. Blood is what the egg needs.
Our men have done their bit, they've gone,
it was all they were good for, poor dears. Now
it is up to us. The egg is quietly screaming
for supper, blood, supper, blood, supper!
Attack, my little Draculas, my Amazons!
Look at those flailing arms and stamping feet.
They're running, swatting, swearing, oh they're hopeless.
Keep at them, ladies. This is a feast.
This is a midsummer night's dream.
Soon we shall all lie down filled and rich,
and lay, and lay, and lay, and lay, and lay.

Bernard McLaverty   I love this poem for its voice – wicked and sly and as urgent as sex. Altogether
malevolent. With antenna-rubbing gestures and snickering, it's the bane of the
Scottish Tourist Board, now called something ridiculous like Comehither Scotland. I
lived on a west coast island for years and can testify to the miseries wrought by this
creature on still wet summer days, kilt or no kilt.

THE MUMMY
(*The Mummy* [of Rameses II] *was met at Orly airport by
Mme Saunier-Seïté.* – News item, Sept. 1976)

– May I welcome Your Majesty to Paris.

– Mm.

– I hope the flight from Cairo was reasonable.

– Mmmmm.

– We have a germ-proof room at the Museum of Man
    where we trust Your Majesty will have peace and quiet.

– Unh-unh.

– I am sorry, but this is necessary.
    Your Majesty's person harbours a fungus.

– Fng fng's, hn?

– Well, it is something attacking your cells.
    Your Majesty is gently deteriorating
    after nearly four thousand years
    becalmed in masterly embalmment.
    We wish to save you from the worm.

– Wrm hrm! Mgh-mgh-mgh.

– Indeed I know it must be distressing
    to a pharaoh and a son of Ra,
    to the excavator of Abu Simbel
    that glorious temple in the rock,
    to the perfecter of Karnak hall,
    to the hammer of the Hittites,
    to the colossus whose colossus

raised in red granite at holy Thebes
sixteen-men-high astounds the desert
shattered, as Your Majesty in life
shattered the kingdom and oppressed the poor
with such lavish grandeur and panache,
to Rameses, to Ozymandias,
to the Louis Quatorze of the Nile,
how bitter it must be to feel
a microbe eat your camphored bands.
But we are here to help Your Majesty.
We shall encourage you to unwind.
You have many useful years ahead.

– M' n'm 'z 'zym'ndias, kng'v kngz!

– Yes yes. Well, Shelley is dead now.
   He was not embalmed. He will not write
   about Your Majesty again.

– T't'nkh'm'n? H'tsh'ps't?
   'khn't'n N'f'rt'ti? Mm? Mm?

– The hall of fame has many mansions.
   Your Majesty may rest assured
   your deeds will always be remembered.

– Youmm w'm'nn. B't'f'lll w'm'nnnn.
   No w'm'nnn f'r th'zndz y'rz.

– Your Majesty, what are you doing?

– Ng! Mm. Mhm. Mm? Mm? Mmmmm.

– Your Majesty, Your Majesty! You'll break your stitches!

– Fng st'chez fng's wrm hrm.

– I really hate to have to use
    a hypodermic on a mummy,
    but we cannot have you strain yourself.
    Remember your fungus, Your Majesty.

– Fng. Zzzzzzz.

– That's right.

– Aaaaaaaah.

Edwin Morgan has the mummy making lots of lust-filled noises at the attractive lady in charge of him – I always laugh out loud when I read it. It is Morgan's sense of humour – subtle, sly, warmly human. Also, it's an unexpected take on what was probably a dry piece of information in a newspaper.

Sheila Templeton

MY DAY AMONG THE CANNONBALLS

Europe is all wars. Its plains are drenched in blood.
Treaties signed, treaties broken, forgotten,
Empires bursting from the gun of history,
Empires burnt out by the fires of history –
Should we worry, sitting here at peace?
Of course not. Yes we should. I don't know.
I know I have fought, have had allegiances,
But I am left with reminiscences,
Which are my best, least understood credentials.
Let me lay one before you. Gather round.
Come on, it's a cracker, you'll not find its like.

My company was stationed 'somewhere in Europe',
I don't remember the name of the grim town
We were besieging. It was well fortified
With gates chains embrasures machicolations
Batteries redouts vigilantes god knows what,
A bristly sort of come-and-get-me place
We had tried in vain to penetrate.
Logic, I said to myself, think logic.
We cannot infiltrate, what's left but up
Up and over, what goes up and over?
A balloon? Don't be silly, they'd shoot it down.
There's only one way, and I should emphasize
I was at the peak of my physical powers –
A long time ago, yes yes I know --
I climbed up onto our biggest cannon
And when the next huge ball began to emerge
I jumped it, like on horseback, and was off

Whizzing into the smoky air. Aha,
I thought, this is how to do it! But then,
Halfway towards the enemy, I wondered:
Would they not catch me, string me up as a spy?
Not good! I must get back, but back how?
Logic again saw just one solution:
Transfer to the next enemy cannonball
Coming towards me: a delicate operation,
But I accomplished it, and so back home.

Not the most glorious of episodes,
I hear you say. Oh but it was, it was!
Was the siege lifted? I really don't know.
Did the enemy surrender? I cannot recall.
What I remember is the exhilaration
Of the ball between my knees like a celestial horse
And the wind whistling its encouragement
And at the high point of my flight an eagle
Shrieking at the usurper of that space
Between ground and sky, between friend and foe,
Between the possible and the impossible.
I shrieked back to the wild bird in my gladness.
What an unearthly duet – but life, life!

The hero decided that the best way to win a siege was to jump onto a cannonball
as it emerged from one of his side's cannons and ride it like a 'celestial horse' over
the town wall. The stupidity of doing so and the inevitability of his being captured
made him transfer to an outgoing cannonball in mid-air. What he remembers is the
exhilaration and gladness. All the poems in *Tales from Baron Munchausen* are full of
a vivid *joie de vivre*.

David Smith

ONE CIGARETTE

No smoke without you, my fire.
After you left,
your cigarette glowed on in my ashtray
and sent up a long thread of such quiet grey
I smiled to wonder who would believe its signal
of so much love. One cigarette
in the non-smoker's tray.
As the last spire
trembles up, a sudden draught
blows it winding into my face.
Is it smell, is it taste?
You are here again, and I am drunk on your tobacco lips.
Out with the light.
Let the smoke lie back in the dark.
Till I hear the very ash
sigh down among the flowers of brass
I'll breathe, and long past midnight, your last kiss.

Liz Cameron   I simply love 'One Cigarette', though in the light of the smoking ban, it's hardly PC to do so now – or at least, hardly healthy! I loved it from the moment I heard Eddie read it at the Glasgow University Literary Society half a lifetime ago. It gave me goose-pimples then and it does now. And it reminds me of relationships and loves recollected now in tranquillity but which left me aching with a mixture of exaltation and anguish at the time.

FOR THE OPENING OF THE SCOTTISH PARLIAMENT, 9 OCTOBER 2004

Open the doors! Light of the day, shine in; light of the mind, shine out!
We have a building which is more than a building.
There is a commerce between inner and outer, between brightness and
  shadow, between the world and those who think about the world.
Is it not a mystery? The parts cohere, they come together like petals of a
  flower, yet they also send their tongues outward to feel and taste
  the teeming earth.
Did you want classic columns and predictable pediments? A growl of old
  Gothic grandeur? A blissfully boring box?
Not here, no thanks! No icon, no IKEA, no iceberg, but curves and
  caverns, nooks and niches, huddles and heavens, syncopations
  and surprises. Leave symmetry to the cemetery.
But bring together slate and stainless steel, black granite and grey
  granite, seasoned oak and sycamore, concrete blond and smooth
  as silk – the mix is almost alive - it breathes and beckons
  – imperial marble it is not!

Come down the Mile, into the heart of the city, past the kirk of St Giles
  and the closes and wynds of the noted ghosts of history who
  drank their claret and fell down the steep tenement stairs into
  the arms of link-boys but who wrote and talked the starry
  Enlightenment of their days –
And before them the auld makars who tickled a Scottish king's ear with
  melody and ribaldry and frank advice –
And when you are there, down there, in the midst of things, not set upon
  an hill with your nose in the air,
This is where you know your parliament should be
And this is where it is, just here.

What do the people want of the place? They want it to be filled with
  thinking persons as open and adventurous as its architecture.
A nest of fearties is what they do not want.
A symposium of procrastinators is what they do not want.
A phalanx of forelock-tuggers is what they do not want.
And perhaps above all the droopy mantra of 'it wizny me' is what they do
  not want.

Dear friends, dear lawgivers, dear parliamentarians, you are picking
up a thread of pride and self-esteem that has been almost but
not quite, oh no not quite, not ever broken or forgotten.

When you convene you will be reconvening, with a sense of not
wholly the power, not yet wholly the power, but a good sense
of what was once in the honour of your grasp.
All right. Forget, or don't forget, the past. Trumpets and robes are
fine, but in the present and the future you will need something
more.
What is it? We, the people, cannot tell you yet, but you will know
about it when we do tell you.
We give you our consent to govern, don't pocket it and ride away.
We give you our deepest dearest wish to govern well, don't say we
have no mandate to be so bold.
We give you this great building, don't let your work and hope be other
than great when you enter and begin.
So now begin. Open the doors and begin.

Paul Scott   It is admirable to find the Scottish Makar giving good, robust advice to the
Parliamentarians, some of it in 'plain, braid Lallans', and especially because he
reminded them that they had 'not yet wholly the power'.

PELAGIUS

I, Morgan, whom the Romans call Pelagius,
Am back in my own place, my green Cathures
By the frisky firth of salmon, by the open sea
Not far, place of my name, at the end of things
As it must seem. But it is not a dream
Those voyages, my hair grew white at the tiller,
I have been where I say I have been,
And my cheek still burns for the world.
That sarcophagus by the Molendinar –
Keep the lid on, I am not stepping into it yet!
I used to think of the grey rain and the clouds
From my hot cave in the Negev, I shooed
The scuttle of scorpions. I had a hat –
You should have seen me – against the sun
At its zenith in that angry Palestine.
I spoke; I had crowds; there was a demon in me.
There had been crowds four centuries before,
And what had come of that? That was the question.
I did not keep back what I had to say.
Some were alarmed. They did not like my red hair.
But I had a corps of friends who shouldered
Every disfavour aside, took ship with me
Westward over the heaving central sea.
We came to Carthage then, and not alone.
The city was seething livid with refugees.
Such scenes, such languages! Such language!
The Goths were in Rome. I saw a master
I had studied under, wild-eyed,
Clutching tattered scrolls, running.
I saw a drift of actors with baskets
Brimming broken masks, they gestured
Bewildered beyond any mime.
I saw a gladiator with half a sword.
I heard a Berber's fiddle twang like the end of a world.
Morgan, I said to myself, take note,

Take heart. In a time of confusion
You must make a stand. There is a chrysalis
Throbbing to disgorge oppression and pessimism,
Proscription, prescription, conscription,
Praying mantises. Cut them down!

One stood against me:
Distinguished turncoat, ex-Manichee, ex this and that,
Preacher of chastity with a son in tow,
A Christian pistoned by new-found fervour,
Born of the desert sand in occupied land,
Born my exact coeval but not my coadjutor,
Bishop in Hippo brandishing anathemas,
Bristling with intelligence not my intelligence,
Black-hearted but indefatigable –
Augustine! You know who you are
And I know who you are and we shall die
Coeval as we came to life coeval.
We are old. The dark is not far off.
It is four hundred years now since those nails
Were hammered in that split the world
And not just flesh. Text and anti-text
Crush the light. You can win,
Will win, I can see that, crowd me out
With power of councils, but me –
Do you know me, can you believe
I have something you cannot have –
My city, not the city of God –
It is to come, and why, do you know why?

Because no one will believe without a splash from a font
Their baby will howl in eternal cold, or fire,
And no one will suffer the elect without merit
To lord it over a cringing flock, and no one
Is doomed by Adam's sin to sin for ever,
And who says Adam's action was a sin,
Or Eve's, when they let history in.

Sometimes when I stand on Blythswood Hill
And strain my eyes (they are old now) to catch
Those changing lights of evening, and the clouds
Going their fiery way towards the firth,
I think we must just be ourselves at last
And wait like prophets – no, not wait, work! –
As prophets do, to see the props dissolve,
The crutches, threats, vain promises,
Altars, ordinances, comminations
Melt off into forgetfulness.
My robe flaps; a gull swoops; man is all.
Cathurian towers will ring this hill.
Engines unheard of yet will walk the Clyde.
I do not even need to raise my arms,
My blessing breathes with the earth.
It is for the unborn, to accomplish their will
With amazing, but only human, grace.

Morgan imagines Pelagius visiting Glasgow, but this is also a self-portrait of the poet, as an old man now, back in the city, going back to the Pelagian heresy. Do you remember the Pelagian heresy? It's the idea that there is no such thing as original sin. There is no original sin. We need not suffer guilt simply because we're human beings and alive. So, transcend guilt! There is so much more to be made of this world, in simply human terms.

Alan Riach

PILATE AT FORTINGALL

A Latin harsh with Aramaicisms
poured from his lips incessantly; it made
no sense, for surely he was mad. The glade
of birches shamed his rags, in paroxysms
he stumbled, toga'd, furred, blear, brittle, grey.
They told us he sat here beneath the yew
even in downpours; ate dog-scraps. Crows flew
from prehistoric stone to stone all day.
'See him now.' He crawled to the cattle-trough
at dusk, jumbled the water till it sloshed
and spilled into the hoof-mush in blue strands,
slapped with useless despair each sodden cuff,
and washed his hands, and watched his hands, and washed
his hands, and watched his hands, and washed his hands.

Lesley Duncan   *The Sonnets from Scotland* are my favourites: their imaginative sweep, from the
deep past to some post-nuclear dispensation, is immensely impressive, as is their
craftsmanship. 'Pilate at Fortingall' shows the poet exercising his prerogative to elide
myth and biblical narrative and to explore, with sympathy, a troubled conscience.

THE RING OF BRODGAR

'If those stones could speak –' Do not wish too loud.
They can, they do, they will. No voice is lost.
Your meanest guilts are bonded in like frost.
Your fearsome sweat will rise and leave its shroud.
I well recall the timeprint of the Ring
of Brodgar we discovered, white with dust
in twenty-second-century distrust
of truth, but dustable, with truths to bring
into the freer ages, as it did.
A thin groan fought the wind that tugged the stones.
It filled an auditorium with pain.
Long was the sacrifice. Pity ran, hid.
Once they heard the splintering of the bones
they switched the playback off, in vain, in vain.

For me it exemplifies so much of what I love in Eddie's poetry, but in this case especially the confident melding of a kind of knuckly geographical, historical realism along with an intense and unsentimental science fictional appreciation of the implications of the inescapable certainty of the future, of what's to come and how it will reassess both the present past and our present as past.

Iain Banks

THE SECOND LIFE

But does every man feel like this at forty –
I mean it's like Thomas Wolfe's New York, his
heady light, the stunning plunging canyons, beauty –
pale stars winking hazy downtown quitting-time,
and the winter moon flooding the skyscrapers, northern –
an aspiring place, glory of the bridges, foghorns
are enormous messages, a looming mastery
that lays its hand on the young man's bowels
until he feels in that air, that rising spirit
all things are possible, he rises with it
until he feels that he can never die –
Can it be like this, and is this what it means
in Glasgow now, writing as the aircraft roar
over building sites, in this warm west light
by the daffodil banks that were never so crowded and lavish –
green May, and the slow great blocks rising
under yellow tower cranes, concrete and glass and steel
out of a dour rubble it was and barefoot children gone –
Is it only the slow stirring, a city's renewed life
that stirs me, could it stir me so deeply
as May, but could May have stirred
what I feel of desire and strength
like an arm saluting a sun?

All January, all February the skaters
enjoyed Bingham's pond, the crisp cold evenings,
they swung and flashed among car headlights,
the drivers parked round the unlit pond
to watch them, and give them light, what laughter
and pleasure rose in the rare lulls
of the yards-away stream of wheels along Great Western Road!
The ice broke up, but the boats came out.
The painted boats are ready for pleasure.
The long light needs no headlamps.

Black oar cuts a glitter: it is heaven on earth.

Is it true that we come alive
not once, but many times?
We are drawn back to the image
of the seed in darkness, or the greying skin
of the snake that hides a shining one –
it will push that used-up matter off
and even the film of the eye is sloughed –
That the world may be the same, and we are not
and so the world is not the same,
the second eye is making again
this place, these waters and these towers,
they are rising again
as the eye stands up to the sun,
as the eye salutes the sun.

Many things are unspoken
in the life of a man, and with a place
there is an unspoken love also
in undercurrents, drifting, waiting its time.
A great place and its people are not renewed lightly.
The caked layers of grime
grow warm, like homely coats.
But yet they will be dislodged
and men will still be warm.
The old coats are discarded.
The old ice is loosed.
The old seeds are awake.

Slip out of darkness, it is time.

As we are carried along on its flow, at first conversationally, then with increasing   David Betteridge
lyricism, we wonder: is this poem about Glasgow or the whole world? About nature
or culture? About the poet or ourselves? We find it is about all of these, marvellously
unified under the aegis of renewal.

SIESTA OF A HUNGARIAN SNAKE

s sz sz SZ sz SZ sz ZS zs ZS zs zs z

THE SPUTNIK'S TALE
(1957 AD)

One day, as I was idling above the earth,
an unexpected glint caught my eye,
whizzing silver, a perky sphere with prongs.
I knew it was time for such things to appear
but this was the first: man-made, well-made,
artificial but a satellite for all that:
a who-goes-there for the universe!
I came closer: the gleaming aluminium
sparkled, hummed, vibrated, its four
spidery antennas had the spring of the newly created.
It seemed a merry creature, even cocky.
It had a voice. I said hello to it.

'Can't stop,' it cried. 'I am in orbit.
Join me if you want to talk. *Beep.*
Travel with me, be the sputnik's sputnik.'
I flew alongside. 'What have you seen?' I asked.
'Wall of China, useless object that.
Continents. Tankers. Deltas like pony-tails.
Collective *beep* farms everywhere. Oh and
the earth like a ball, mustn't forget that,
proof positive. And a blue glow
all round it if you like such *beep* things.'

'You haven't always been bound in a bit of metal?'
I asked. 'Damn sure I *beep* haven't,' he replied,
colour chasing colour across his surface.
'I was a bard in the barbarous times,
Widsith the far-traveller. The world was my mead-hall.
Goths gave me gold. I blossomed in Burgundy.
I watched Picts prick *beep* patterns on themselves.
I sang to Saracens for a sweet supper.
I shared the floor with a shaman in Finland.
Good is the giver who helps the harper!'

'I have nothing to give you,' I said,
'but truth. You have three months to live
in this orbit, and then you are a cinder.'
He darkened. 'You may well be right.'
But remembering Widsith he flushed into tremulous light.
'We'll see. *Beep.* We'll see. *Beep.* We'll see.'

Gwyneth Lewis   Who else but Edwin Morgan could imagine the Russian satellite Sputnik as the reincarnation of an ancient poet? Perhaps the quality I love most about Edwin Morgan's work is the combination of comedy and high seriousness. It's entirely typical of his talent that he has Sputnik speaking like your next-door-neighbour would, busy on the way to the shops. I also love the way that Sputnik's radio signals become the metre of the poem, like a hiccup in its way of talking, so that the last line becomes an almost abstract mantra: 'We'll see. *Beep.* We'll see. *Beep.* We'll see.'

THE STARLINGS IN GEORGE SQUARE

I

Sundown on the high stonefields!
The darkening roofscape stirs –
thick – alive with starlings
gathered singing in the square –
like a shower of arrows they cross
the flash of a western window,
they bead the wires with jet,
they nestle preening by the lamps
and shine, sidling by the lamps
and sing, shining, they stir
the homeward hurrying crowds.
A man looks up and points
smiling to his son beside him
wide-eyed at the clamour on those cliffs –
it sinks, shrills out in waves,
levels to a happy murmur,
scatters in swooping arcs,
a stab of confused sweetness
that pierces the boy like a story,
a story more than a song.
He will never forget that evening,
the silhouette of the roofs,
the starlings by the lamps.

II

The City Chambers are hopping mad.
Councillors with rubber plugs in their ears!
Secretaries closing windows!
Window-cleaners want protection and danger money.
The Lord Provost can't hear herself think, man.
What's that?
Lord Provost, can't hear herself think.

At the General Post Office
the clerks write Three Pounds Starling in the savings-books.
Each telephone-booth is like an aviary.
I tried to send a parcel to County Kerry but –
The cables to Cairo got fankled, sir.
What's that?
I said the cables to Cairo got fankled.
And as for the City Information Bureau –
I'm sorry I can't quite chirrup did you twit –
No I wanted to twee but perhaps you can't cheep –
Would you try once again, that's better, I – sweet –
When's the last boat to Milngavie? Tweet?
What's that?
I said when's the last boat to Milngavie?

III

There is nothing for it now but scaffolding:
clamp it together, send for the bird-men,
Scarecrow Strip for the window-ledge landings,
Cameron's Repellent on the overhead wires.
Armour our pediments against eavesdroppers.
This is a human outpost. Save our statues.
Send back the jungle. And think of the joke:
as it says in the papers, It is very comical
to watch them alight on the plastic rollers
and take a tumble. So it doesn't kill them?
All right, so who's complaining? This isn't Peking
where they shoot the sparrows for hygiene and cash.
So we're all humanitarians, locked in our cliff-dwellings
encased in our repellent, guano-free and guilt-free.
The Lord Provost sings in her marble hacienda.
The Postmaster-General licks an audible stamp.
Sir Walter is vexed that his column's deserted.
I wonder if we really deserve starlings?

There is something to be said for these joyous messengers
that we repel in our indignant orderliness.
They lift up the eyes, they lighten the heart,
and some day we'll decipher that sweet frenzied whistling
as they wheel and settle along our hard roofs
and take those grey buttresses for home.
One thing we know they say, after their fashion.
They like the warm cliffs of man.

I've enjoyed Edwin Morgan's poems for years – my favourite is probably 'The Starlings in George Square'. It really did happen! I remember so well as a child my dad telling me about the starling problem and how the great civic minds in the City Chambers were exercised in finding a solution. I like the way the poem is written in three parts, each different but painting such wonderful pictures.

Linda Fabiani

STRAWBERRIES

There were never strawberries
like the ones we had
that sultry afternoon
sitting on the step
of the open french window
facing each other
your knees held in mine
the blue plates in our laps
the strawberries glistening
in the hot sunlight
we dipped them in sugar
looking at each other
not hurrying the feast
for one to come
the empty plates
laid on the stone together
with the two forks crossed
and I bent towards you
sweet in that air
in my arms
abandoned like a child
from your eager mouth
the taste of strawberries
in my memory
lean back again
let me love you

let the sun beat
on our forgetfulness
one hour of all
the heat intense
and summer lightning
on the Kilpatrick hills

let the storm wash the plates

Stewart Conn   In its economy of setting and deceptive simplicity of expression, how evocative and sensuous it is from the outset, and how subtly sustained the alliterative pattern of 's' and 'st' sounds pinning its two-beat lines in place. But it is the last line which touchingly clinches things, both at a practical, almost mundane level and in conjuring up, in the intense heat, an alternative urgency. I sense in it a reminder of how moments of intimacy must be grasped, in the face not just of the elements but of mortality.

SUNDAY IN EAST MARS

Poems come from East Mars, said Spicer,
and so they do. Our most perjink transmitters,
miniaturised to the last murmur, for protection
against not only probes but all explorers,
push our particles of that strenuous pleasure
you do your best to record. Intermittent
the bursts are, not to be taken for granted.
We want you to know, and not to manage.
We think you manage far too much. We'd never
send you a scenario, a storyboard, a legend,
but we do and in our own time endlessly will
give you signals that show greater power's
in stories than in story. What is adjustment?
Giving up. What is a whole? A sum of
parts done wrong. Oh if outgrowing of concepts –
we tap our keys with some fervour here – is dolphins
that slice the air into dripping arcs, figureheads
brighter than any boat was ever fixed to,
we think we've seen inexplicable helpers
that might sustain a castaway. Delight is use
and use delight, and when you write you
move the shape of things that millimetre
it needs to breathe, be reassured of living,
not that it was ever not living, but flickers
and shiftings of its great mass are so sanative
it grows, re-forms yet never forms, advances
in its own dimensions.
                              It is like a Sunday
here. We are very calm. Scarlet nasturtiums
twine with vigorous will between the boulders.
I love to watch them when I'm not transmitting.
We'll send you one, but then you have it, don't you?

The SciFi genre is often the occasion for a writer to lay out a dystopian vision of the future, but in Morgan's hands it's quite the opposite. The future, filled with gadgetry and the rise of machines is for him an occasion for opportunity, excitement and celebration. There's a profound faith there in the nub of what makes (and will keep) us human, despite technology. So it is with this poem, where the machines ('Our most perjink transmitters') act as a means to explore the sources of poetry and the poet's art.

Marc Lambert

TESTAMENT

Through the storm he walked before he gave his sermon.
The sails were whipped to shreds. He took a turn.
There was hardly any air not dense with spray,
they choked as they half saw him out there
going or coming, who knows, through the sea-lumps.
His face was like a sheet of lightning. 'Beside him,
his injured arm in a sling, was Red Nelson,
his sou-wester gone and his fair hair plastered in wet,
wind-blown ringlets about his face. His whole attitude
breathed indomitability, courage, strength.
It seemed almost as though the divine
were blazing forth from him.' They shipped water,
baled, shipped water, baled, baled, baled.
Things blew themselves out. They tottered to shore,
too busy to see him back on board,
though he'd baled, he told them. There was no sermon.
They dried their rags on stones, he kept his on,
sitting a little apart, his sou'wester gone
and his fair hair plastered in wet, wind-blown
ringlets about his face. His whole attitude breathed
indomitability, courage, strength. It seemed
almost as though the divine were blazing forth from him.

They asked me to write this faithfully.
I do, and yet I am not sure that I do.
Sometimes I frown at what the pen has said.
My understanding breaks in waves, dissolves.
I am tired of walking on the sea.
Give me ice or vapour, terra firma,
some change that is a change not a betrayal.
Water would be water even with footprints
soldered to it in characters of fire
– as they were that day – God knows – as they were!

James McGonigal   I like this poem's mystery, and its guarded then unguarded witness statement about
mystery. It speaks to EM's lifelong argument with Christianity, threaded through his
work. I like the way the quote is unexplained. The washed-out rags and patches on
the shore of belief also appeal, and its manifestation of power and powerlessness.

TO JOAN EARDLEY

Pale yellow letters
humbly straggling across
the once brilliant red
of a broken shop-face
CONFECTIO
and a blur of children
at their games, passing,
gazing as they pass
at the blur of sweets
in the dingy, cosy
Rottenrow window –
an Eardley on my wall.
Such rags and streaks
that master us! –
that fix what the pick
and bulldozer have crumbled
to a dingier dust,
the living blur
fiercely guarding
energy that has vanished,
cries filling still
the unechoing close!
I wandered by the rubble
and the houses left standing
kept a chill, dying life
in their islands of stone.
No window opened
as the coal cart rolled
and the coalman's call
fell coldly to the ground.
But the shrill children
jump on my wall.

I love best this little raggedy poem, boldly textured and richly coloured as the gem of an Eardley still hanging beside Morgan as he writes.

Rosaleen Orr

TRIO

Coming up Buchanan Street, quickly, on a sharp winter evening
a young man and two girls, under the Christmas lights –
The young man carries a new guitar in his arms,
the girl on the inside carries a very young baby,
and the girl on the outside carries a chihuahua.
And the three of them are laughing, their breath rises
in a cloud of happiness, and as they pass
the boy says, 'Wait till he sees this but!'
The chihuahua has a tiny Royal Stewart tartan coat like a teapot-
 holder,
the baby in its white shawl is all bright eyes and mouth like favours in
 a fresh sweet cake,
the guitar swells out under its milky plastic cover, tied at the neck
 with silver tinsel tape and a brisk sprig of mistletoe.
Orphean sprig! Melting baby! Warm chihuahua!
The vale of tears is powerless before you.
Whether Christ is born, or is not born, you
put paid to fate, it abdicates under the Christmas lights.
Monsters of the year
go blank, are scattered back,
can't bear this march of three.
– And the three have passed, vanished in the crowd
(yet not vanished, for in their arms they wind
the life of men and beasts, and music,
laughter ringing them round like a guard)
at the end of this winter's day.

Richard Holloway   I like it because it captures the best of the strange season of Christmas. Preachers inveigh against it as having been commercialised out of its original meaning, but this poem, in a deeply humanistic and secular way, captures the essence of the festival, which is about the gift of love, the best of us.

Patricia Sutherland   It shows how the ordinary can be transformed into something significant and life-enhancing, and it's about the human capacity for joy. This wintry Buchanan Street strikes a chord with every Glaswegian, but its affirmation of the power of human love and laughter is for everyone.

A VIEW OF THINGS

what I love about dormice is their size
what I hate about rain is its sneer
what I love about the Bratach Gorm is its unflappability
what I hate about scent is its smell
what I love about newspapers is their etaoin shrdl
what I hate about philosophy is its pursed lip
what I love about Rory is his old grouse
what I hate about Pam is her pinkie
what I love about semi-precious stones is their preciousness
what I hate about diamonds is their mink
what I love about poetry is its ion engine
what I hate about hogs is their setae
what I love about love is its porridge-spoon
what I hate about hate is its eyes
what I love about hate is its salts
what I hate about love is its dog
what I love about Hank is his string vest
what I hate about the twins is their three gloves
what I love about Mabel is her teeter
what I hate about gooseberries is their look, feel, smell, and taste
what I love about the world is its shape
what I hate about a gun is its lock, stock, and barrel
what I love about bacon-and-eggs is its predictability
what I hate about derelict buildings is their reluctance to disintegrate
what I love about a cloud is its unpredictability
what I hate about you, chum, is your china
what I love about many waters is their inability to quench love

A WATER HORSE

Impossibly a totality of water
dragonlike some force must surely have uttered
creature from underground chaos emerging
shook itself loose of almost clovelike grits and
grouts and with such thrustful bunched mounting
of air as made a bellying of night-clouds
rose glittering and bucketing over mountains
till at last the moon the unconscionable rider
tugged its unbridled hide and slowly cantered
across the universe, a shine upon a
shine, a whinny from a throat of water.

WHEN YOU GO

When you go,
if you go,
and I should want to die,
there's nothing I'd be saved by
more than the time
you fell asleep in my arms
in a trust so gentle
I let the darkening room
drink up the evening, till
rest, or the new rain
lightly roused you awake.
I asked if you heard the rain in your dream
and half dreaming still you only said, I love you.

THE WORLD

1

I don't think it's not going onward,
though no one said it was a greyhound.
I don't accept we're wearing late.

I don't see the nothing some say anything
that's not in order comes to be found.
It may be nothing to be armour-plated.

I don't believe that what's been made
clutters the spirit. Let it be patented
and roll. It never terrorized

three ikon angels sitting at a table
in Moscow, luminous as a hologram
and blessing everything from holograms

to pliers at a dripping nail.
I don't believe it's not the wrench
of iron that let the body fall.

2

There was this unholy scuffle.
They felled the sober with the tipsy.
At last someone got pushed mildly

onto a breadknife. As he observed
in the ward, What's more, what's more,
just nobody's going to go there.

They did though. Even if which was which
was always a guessing-game, the case
meant the whole scene had bristles on.

Expressionless hardmen glittered. Sleepwalkers
jived. There was a dog. Before
the end of the evening a desire

for everything had returned, very
smoky it's true, but true. The sleeper
in the ward was the only one with nightmares.

                      3
Sometimes it swells like the echo of a passion
dying with paeans, not sighs. Who
knows the weight and list of its rebellions?

Underneath, underneath, underneath, underneath –
you think it beats in the age-old fashion,
even red, perhaps, like a pre-set strawberry

creeping below the crust? It's artistic
to have ordered impulses. To
think the world has makes you feel great.

Beyond the world, the slow-dying sun
flares out a signal fan, projecting
a million-mile arm in skinny hydrogen

to flutter it at our annals.
Coarse, knee-deep in years, we
go on counting, miss the vast unreason.

                      4
Technologies like dragonflies, the strange
to meet the strange; and at the heart
of things, who knows what is dependent?

Imagine anything the world could, it might
do; anything not to do, it would.
A plume of act flies as it spins by.

We saw the nettles in the ancient station.
The signalbox was like a windmill, haunted
by bats and autumn wasps. She

twirled a scarf through leaves. Remembrance
offered nothing, swam in our hands.
We're here. The past is not our home.

I don't think it's not being perfect
that brings the sorrows in, but being soon
beyond the force not to be powerless.

John Burnside   I'd like to note in passing the clarity and honesty of 'One Cigarette' – surely one of the best love poems ever written in these islands – before settling upon 'The World', partly because it encompasses so many of the virtues for which Edwin Morgan is so admired and loved, but mostly because – having earned the right to do so with a perfect balance of lyricism and quiet rhetoric – the last lines always move me to a place beyond any kind of philosophy, a place beyond thought or hope or acceptance or grief or tears, no matter how often I read this great poem.

HISTORICAL NOTES

Boethius, Anicius Manlius Severinus (c.475-524), Roman statesman and philosopher; wrote *On the Consolation of Philosophy (De Consolatione Philosophiae)* in prison.

Eardley, Joan (1921-63), Sussex-born painter, worked in Scotland.

Hopkins, Gerard Manley (1844-89), English priest and poet.

McGinn, Matt (1928-77), Glasgow singer and songwriter.

Pelagius (c.355-c.425), British theologian, his name a Greek translation of the Celtic 'Morgan'; considered heretical for denying original sin.

Pilatus, Pontius, Roman procurator of Judaea (26-36), oversaw the execution of Jesus.

Tennant, John (1796-1878), Scottish chemist and industrialist.

Wallace, Sir William (c.1274-1305), Guardian of Scotland.

BIOGRAPHY

Born Glasgow in April 1920, Edwin Morgan has lived in Glasgow all his life, except for service with the RAMC in the Middle East during the Second World War, and his poetry is grounded in the city. He retired from Glasgow University as titular Professor of English in 1980, serving as Glasgow's first Poet Laureate 1999-2002. The title of his 1973 collection, *From Glasgow to Saturn*, suggests the range of Morgan's subject matter. He is the first to hold the post of 'Scots Makar', created by the Scottish Executive in 2004 to recognise the achievement of Scottish poets throughout the centuries. His latest collections include *Tales from Baron Munchausen* (Mariscat Press, 2005), and *A Book of Lives* (Carcanet Press, 2007), which was shortlisted for the T.S. Eliot Prize.

SOURCES FOR THE POEMS

This list shows the books by Edwin Morgan in which the poems first appeared and in which they are reprinted, to give some idea of where they fit in the canon. Those poems included in his *Collected Poems* and *New Selected Poems* indicate their author's regard for them. The poems span most of Edwin Morgan's poetic career, from the 1960s to 2007.

ABOL: *A Book of Lives* (Carcanet, 2007). C: *Cathures* (Carcanet/Mariscat, 2002). CP: *Collected Poems* (Carcanet,1990). D: *Demon* (Mariscat, 1999). FGTS: *From Glasgow to Saturn* (Carcanet,1973). G/T: *Grafts/Takes* (Mariscat, 1983). HHATA: *Hold Hands among the Atoms* (Mariscat,1991). IP: *Instamatic Poems* (Ian McKelvie, 1972). LAAL: *Love and a Life* (Mariscat, 2003). NSP: *New Selected Poems* (Carcanet, 2000). PMP: *Penguin Modern Poets 15* (Penguin, 1969). POTY: *Poems of Thirty Years* (Carcanet, 1982). SFS: *Sonnets from Scotland* (Mariscat, 1984). SOTD: *Sweeping out the Dark* (Carcanet, 1994). TFBM: *Tales from Baron Munchausen* (Mariscat, 2005). TND: *The New Divan* (Carcanet, 1977). TSL: *The Second Life* (Edinburgh University Press, 1968). TWM: *The Wallace Muse* (Luath, 2005). VAOR: *Virtual and Other Realities* (Carcanet,1997)

After a Lecture (LAAL/ABOL). The Apple's Song (FGTS/CP/NSP). Boethius (ABOL). Canedolia (TSL/CP/NSP). Christmas Eve (FGTS/CP). Cinquevalli (POTY/CP/NSP). The Coals (POTY/CP/NSP). The Coin (SFS/CP/NSP). The Computer's First Christmas Card (TSL/CP/NSP). Death in Duke Street (FGTS/CP/NSP). The Death of Marilyn Monroe (TSL/CP/NSP). A Demon (D/C). The First Men on Mercury (FGTS/CP/NSP). The Flowers of Scotland (PMP/CP/NSP). The Freshet (C). From a City Balcony (TSL/CP/NSP). Glasgow 5 March 1971 (IP/CP/NSP). G.M. Hopkins in Glasgow (SFS/CP/NSP). Hyena (FGTS/CP/NSP). In the Snack-Bar (TSL/CP/NSP). Instructions to an Actor (POTY/CP/NSP). John Tennant (C). King Billy (TSL/CP/NSP). The Loch Ness Monster's Song (FGTS/CP/NSP). Lines for Wallace (TWM/ABOL). Making a Poem (CP). Matt McGinn (SFS/CP/NSP). Message Clear (TSL/CP/NSP). Midge (VAOR). The Mummy (POTY/CP/NSP). My Day among the Cannonballs (TFBM). One Cigarette (TSL/CP/NSP). Open the Doors! (ABOL). Pelagius (C). Pilate at Fortingall (SFS/CP/NSP). The Ring of Brodgar (SFS/CP/NSP). The Second Life (TSL/CP/NSP) Siesta of a Hungarian Snake (TSL/CP/NSP). The Sputnik's Tale (ABOL). The Starlings in George Square (TSL/CP/NSP). Strawberries (TSL/CP/NSP). Sunday in East Mars (HHATA/SOTD). Testament (G/T). To Joan Eardley (TSL/CP/NSP). Trio (TSL/CP/NSP). A View of Things (TSL/CP/NSP). A Water Horse (HHATA/SOTD). When You Go (TSL/CP/NSP). The World (TND/CP/NSP).